INTRODUCTION

Hi! Welcome to the wonderful world of herps!

No, herps are not a disease—they're reptiles and amphibians. Those of us who love the scaly or slimy critters of the world got tired of calling them "reptiles and amphibians" all the time, so someone coined *herps* as a slang term—it's a lot shorter. The study of reptiles and amphibians is

A young adult leopard gecko, *Eublepharis macularius*. An odd feature visible here is that light can pass all the way through the gecko's head via the ear openings. Photo by M. Gilroy.

called *herpetology*, so it seemed natural to call our animals herps.

There! You already know an "insider" term. (We'll get to the secret handshake later.) And I consider you an insider because you wouldn't have even picked up this book if you feared herps, as so many do. Not everyone can see the beauty in a lizard, snake, frog, or other herp...and I think that the people who can are special.

A very beautiful herp is the one we'll cover in this small volume—the leopard gecko. Not only is it pretty, but it is very easy to keep. I believe it is the perfect first pet lizard.

The goal of this book is simple: by the time we're done here, I hope to teach you everything you need to know to keep and breed leopard geckos. I will try to keep things simple, but there will be new terms and ideas to learn. I'll explain as we go.

But there is also a secondary goal. I want you to discover that herps are fun pets. For those of you who have never kept a herp before, I think that you will enjoy leopard geckos so much that you will eventually want to keep other herps as well.

So let's dive right in now, and once again, welcome to the herp club.

JUST WHAT IS A GECKO ANYWAY?

We're going to get just a little bit technical here. Don't be scared! Altogether, the geckos are a family of lizards called Gekkonidae (pronounced gek-CON-eh-day). The word *gecko* is probably an attempt to describe the sounds that many species make—little barks and squeaks. Most geckos are nocturnal (active at night) and have no movable eyelids, but only a spectacle, a transparent scale that protects the eye. Because they're nocturnal, most geckos have elliptical pupils, like a cat. Most geckos also have flat toe pads covered with microscopic hooks that let them climb easily, tive than the climbing geckos. Leopards do have the "cat eyes," though. The leopard geckos and their close relatives, such as the banded geckos of North and Central America and the fat-tailed geckos of Africa, form the subfam-

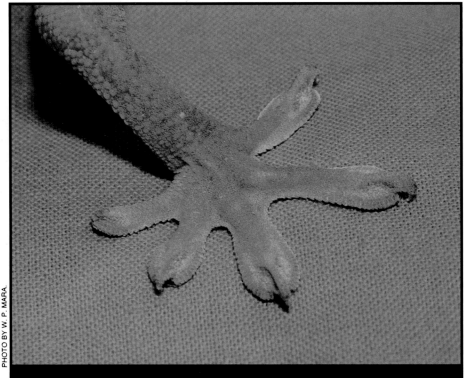

PHOTO BY W. P. MARA.

The foot of a typical gecko is flattened and enables the lizard to climb well. Eyelid geckos such as leopard geckos do **not** have this feature, and are generally poor climbers.

even running up a glass window or upside-down on a ceiling. Geckos are thought to be among the most primitive lizards alive today.

Now that I've told you what geckos are, forget it! Well, most of it, anyway—because leopard geckos and their relatives aren't like the rest of the geckos. The leopard gecko has movable eyelids and no toe pads. This makes the leopard geckos even more primi-

ily Eublepharinae (say it: you-bleh-FAIR-eh-nay). This Latin name translates roughly as "true eyelid," so most herp keepers call these the "eyelid geckos." The leopard gecko goes by the scientific name of *Eublepharis macularius* (you-bleh-FAIR-iss mac-you-LAIR-ee-us). The word *macularius* means "spotted," and so the whole name of our little critter translates as "spotted eyelid gecko." Not bad, but "leopard gecko" does have a bit more zip, doesn't it?

Leopard geckos come from India and Pakistan. They inhabit deserts and arid grasslands, and often take shelter under rocks or

specimens of about 8 inches, counting the tail, are more usual.

Speaking of the tail, leopard geckos and a lot of other lizards have an unusual defense mechanism. The tail breaks off easily if

PHOTO BY K. H. SWITAK.

This view of a reticulated gecko, *Coleonyx reticulatus*, shows the movable eyelids possessed by all eublepharine geckos.

in burrows that they may or may not dig themselves. While dry, these regions are not as parched as deserts like the Sahara, and this will become important as we examine housing requirements in a later chapter. The vast majority of the leopard geckos seen in pet shops today are captive-bred, not wild, but their ancestors were largely from the Pakistan population. Leopard geckos have been known to reach 10 inches, but

pressure is applied to it, and it will squirm a bit after snapping off. This is called *autotomy*. It is assumed that this might distract a predator and give the lizard a chance to escape. In leopard geckos the tail is pinched in a bit at the base, and this is where it will break. The blood vessels at this point are designed to seal off immediately after the break. The tail will grow back, but it is never quite as nice-looking as the origi-

PHOTO BY K. T. NEMURAS.

This leopard gecko has a regrown tail. A regrown tail is shorter and fatter than the original, and also has a finer texture.

nal. Regrown tails are wider but about half the length of "original equipment" tails, and are also uneven in color and texture. Losing the tail does not hurt the gecko unless it is a lean time for food, because the lizard stores fat in the tail that can be used as an emergency food supply. In fact, recent research shows that in some lizards that use the tail for fat storage, the lizard will resist losing the tail if food is scarce.

Leopard geckos are very pretty lizards. As babies they have purplish-brown and light yellow bands. As they grow, the dark bands start to break up into dots—the spots of the leopard. A few adults will retain traces of the banded pattern, but only a little. There are two basic color varieties being bred today: brown, and "high yellow." The brown variety has a background of dark beige,

sometimes with a hint of purple, over which the spots are superimposed. The high yellow variety has a bright yellow ground color. On a few of these animals there will even be some orange spots. No albinos are known at the present time. Only recently have leopard geckos been bred in quantity, though, and you can bet that there will be some surprises as we continue to breed and enhance them.

Leopard geckos feed largely on insects and other "bugs." Known food items in the wild include beetles, centipedes, scorpions, and spiders. They are very adaptable, though, and will attempt to eat almost any small animal they can successfully cram down. The inherent adaptability of the leopard gecko is precisely what makes it a great pet.

CHOOSING A LEOPARD GECKO

Fortunately, it is relatively easy to select a healthy leopard gecko. This is due in no small part to the fact that most of the leopard geckos available today are captive-bred.

With any herp, leopard geckos included, the first features you want to look at are the eyes. They should be full and bright, with no

Healthy leopard geckos are alert and inquisitive. Photo by M. Gilroy.

crusty deposits at the corners. If the eyes appear sunken, or if they're cloudy, or if the gecko appears unable or unwilling to open its eyes, it might have a problem.

Look at the mouth. Make sure there are no abrasions at the tip of the snout or any cheesy-looking tissue. These are sure signs of mouth rot.

Make sure the lizard is well fed. Leopard geckos are fairly chunky little lizards, and they should not be noticeably skinny. The tail should be quite fat-looking. Geckos that are starving have slender tails, and you can often see ribs and the ridge of the backbone. The legs may be spindly, and you might even be able to see the outlines of the hip bones. A lizard like this is at death's door, and can rarely be saved. It might be a hard thing to do, but don't buy such a lizard out of pity—the odds that you can save it are not good.

Be sure to check the gecko's body for signs of injury. Completely re-grown tails are not a problem, but you might want to pass on a gecko that has very recently broken its tail and still has a scab at the break point. Infection is a possibility.

Check limbs for missing toes or feet. This often happens if at some point the lizards have gotten into fights with others of their own kind. While you're at it, check for any swellings of the digits that might indicate infection. Localized bacterial infections in the feet can also cause toes to drop off.

Look for signs of external parasites—ticks and mites. Both dig in beneath the scales and suck

PHOTO BY M. GILROY.

The skin of a leopard gecko has a pebbled texture.

margins of the scales. Ticks are fond of folds in the skin, so they are usually found around the bases of the legs. Don't buy a lizard with these annoying parasites.

If the lizard is having digestive problems of some sort, you can often see dried fecal material around the vent.

I can sum up by simply saying that a healthy leopard gecko should have clear eyes, clear skin, a robust body, and should be active, alert, and responsive. Pass up any lizard that doesn't show these characteristics.

If you follow the above tips, you should end up with a happy, healthy gecko. However, if it's just not your day and you somehow ended up with an ailing gecko, there's still hope. Turn to the "Health" chapter and we'll go into the treatments for some of the more common ailments of leopard geckos.

HANDLING

For the most part, you should try to handle your leopard gecko as little as possible. Don't get me wrong here; they almost never bite and usually do get very tame and will allow you to handle them, but handling increases the chance of accidents, especially the chance of breaking the tail. That wasp-waist constriction at the base of the tail will break the tail loose with only a little but of pressure, such as accidentally getting the gecko's tail caught

blood, and if present they are easiest to see if you turn the lizard over and look at the whitish belly scales. Mites are about the size of salt grains and are usually red but sometimes brownish. Ticks are really just giant mites, and they will produce pimple-like bumps as they push beneath the between a couple of fingers as it walks over your hand. Be very careful about letting your gecko walk on your clothing, because it is easy for the lizard to snag its claws in the fabric, and it is also very easy for even a fine thread to get wrapped around a toe and cut off the circulation.

your thumb and index finger and curl your other fingers under the abdomen to give it some support. Do not restrain the tail in any way, or you'll break it! When you're done with the lizard, place it upright on the sand and quickly let go. The gecko should immediately run away.

PHOTO BY G. DINGERKUS.

Leopard geckos do not have toe pads, but they do have claws that give them good traction and enable them to climb rough surfaces such as rocks and branches.

If you have to move your lizard for some reason, such as to do some routine cage cleaning or to move one lizard to another enclosure for mating purposes, etc., I recommend that you gently chase the lizard into a small can or jar rather than picking it up yourself.

There are times, though, when you will have to actually handle your leopard gecko. One example I can think of is when it comes time to sex them and you have to roll them over to examine the vent carefully. Grasp the lizard very carefully behind the head with

I'm going to say one more time that you should handle your lizard as little as necessary. Even when you are as gentle as possible, this is a source of stress to the lizard. Stress is a poorly understood phenomenon in reptiles. To give just one example, reptiles that do not eat even when given the correct foods and habitat conditions are often suffering from stress. I know you're proud of your gecko, but resist the temptation to chase it out and pick it up to show off whenever guests arrive.

HOUSING LEOPARD GECKOS

A cage for leopard geckos can be surprisingly simple, but it can also become an attractive highlight to a room with little effort. A 10-gallon aquarium is an inexpensive and easily available enclosure for housing one gecko, or a pair at the most. Let's go over the setup of the 10-gallon terrarium from start to finish, and then we'll consider a few larger setups.

THE SUBSTRATE

The substrate is what's on the bottom of the cage. The odds of any two herp hobbyists agreeing completely on substrate choices are about the same as two people agreeing on pizza toppings. Some prefer to keep their leopard geckos and other herps on plain newspaper. This has the major advantage of being very easy to clean, but it's not very attractive. Others use the

PHOTO COURTESY OF I. FRANCAIS

The proper setup for a leopard gecko includes a heat source, hide box, substrate, and water bowl.

THE TANK

There are still a few old metal-framed, slate-bottomed tanks out there, but I'd advise avoiding them for a couple of reasons: first, they're heavy, and second, they can be difficult to clean completely should the need arise. Dirt and other contaminants can work their way down between the seams. So save yourself the trouble and spring for a nice, new all-glass tank. You'll find it very inexpensive.

indoor/outdoor carpeting commonly known as "astroturf." Again, it's easy to clean—hose it off, dry it, and you're ready to go. I worry about two things with this substrate, however: first, that bits of the plastic "grass" may be eaten accidentally and cause gastric blockage, and second, that the substrate may be too abrasive for the relatively delicate feet and bellies of the geckos (Ask a football player about astroturf burns!).

Corncob bedding is another commonly used herp substrate, but it is really too coarse for leopard geckos. So is gravel, in my opinion. Some have successfully used dry bark mulch as a substrate, but if you opt for this you must avoid cedar mulch or shavings. That stuff is fine for

silica play sand sold for use in children's sandboxes is safe and inert.

It may come as a surprise the first time you see it, but your gecko will eat sand! The reasons for this are not certain. Some feel that it is not normal at all (I disagree), and some believe that the

PHOTO COURTESY OF J. LOLL

In a naturalistic terrarium, cholla wood and rock caves take the place of less decorative hide boxes.

hamsters, but reptiles are irritated by the cedar oil and its strong aroma.

Which leaves us with sand. Some herp people really dislike sand as a substrate, but I have often used it and have never had a reptile health problem that could be blamed on it—not to say that it's impossible. Furthermore, for leopard geckos it's a natural, attractive substrate. It also gives the geckos a chance to dig, which some of them like to do.

About an inch of sand on the bottom of the cage is plenty. The sand should be fine-grained; the

sand may aid digestion by providing an additional source of minerals (calcium!) and perhaps also to grind up the food in much the same way as the gizzard stones of a chicken. I have noticed that the amount of sand ingested increases when sufficient food is not available. Geckos that have been starved may produce stools consisting entirely of sand. It is likely that geckos that eat sand to this degree are doing their best to make up for dietary deficiencies. When they eat this much, however, gut impaction and death often follow.

Since some sand-eating seems to be normal, use it to your advantage. I like to add a cup or so of fine coral sand, which is mostly calcium carbonate, per five pounds of silica sand. Mix the two types of sand evenly. Now, when your gecko feels the urge to chomp a few grains of sand, it'll get some calcium in the bargain. (See the chapter on food & water for more details on why calcium is so important.)

probably does in more herps than any other cause.

If you want to keep your cage simple, you can simply provide a "hidebox." A box of cardboard or plastic, some 4-5 inches square and about 2 inches high, will do nicely. A rounded opening about one inch high and 1.5 inches wide will let the gecko come and go at will. Place the hide box in a corner of the cage. You can easily construct a hidebox yourself, but

PHOTO BY G. & C. MERKER, COURTESY OF J. BERGMAN

Calcium-based sands are thought to provide some calcium to the gecko and pose less risk of impaction than normal sand.

A PLACE TO HIDE

A leopard gecko needs a dark and quiet place to call home. Being nocturnal, leopard geckos will spend most of the day in this refuge, and if deprived of it they will be very stressed-out. They will pace about restlessly, rarely sleep, and will soon stop eating, lose weight, and die. This is stress. If you thought that stress was only something that made S & L presidents jump off of bridges, you're wrong. Stress affects animals too, and it's an invisible killer that

there are boxes manufactured specifically with herps in mind that may be purchased at your local pet shop.

You may want something a bit more natural-looking than a hidebox, and this means constructing caverns and terraces with rocks and wood. Flat pieces of slate or sandstone are probably the easiest rocks to work with because you can stack them to create the shady hollows that geckos like. Once you've come up with a rock arrangement that you like, I strongly advise that you secure the rocks to each other with a bit of aquarium silicone cement. Otherwise, your gecko may accidentally undermine a rock in the course of doing a little digging and cause a fatal cave-in.

Several types of wood are easy to work with, and you can get them at your pet shop. One type commonly sold for reptiles is light-colored logs honeycombed with holes. This is actually the dried "skeleton" of the cholla (pronounced CHOY-ah) cactus. This is attractive, but you should not use it alone because its porous nature makes it a poor shelter. Much better is cork bark, which is sold in interesting-looking planks and gnarly chunks. It is dark in color but light in weight and easily carved if necessary.

Another sort of material that makes good gecko shelters is PVC pipe. The T-shaped pieces, about 2 inches in diameter and with all but one of the openings capped off, are easy to work with. You can even bury them partially in the sand or hide them behind rocks. I'll admit that PVC doesn't look very natural, but it is easily sterilized with mild soap and hot water—not something that can be said about some of the other materials. You can also use stacks of piping to stratify

Small logs are good pieces of decor in a leopard gecko terrarium, and the lizards will often climb about on them. Photo by M. Gilroy.

the space in the cage to allow you to keep more than one gecko in the same enclosure (females only, or one male and several females—NEVER two males).

PHOTO COURTESY OF R. D. BARTLETT

Once a rarity, albino leopard geckos have been bred in large numbers and, consequently, the prices have dropped.

PLANTS

You can keep things simple and not use any plants in your gecko terrarium, but if you like the added decoration there's no reason not to have them. The goal is to pick plant varieties that will do well in the arid terrarium and that will not harm your leopard gecko. Sharp-spined cacti are not a good idea. They do look good, and they are very hardy, but they can injure a gecko. Let's look at a few of the plants that are a bit safer.

Living stones, *Lithops* species, really do look like rocks. Most are about an inch across and do well in well-drained grit under bright light. Water them very infrequently; most people kill these plants with kindness.

Stone roses, *Echeveria*, and the similar-looking *Kleinia* also do well. These are tough-leafed plants that can be treated like the *Lithops*. Water them very little in the wintertime and only a little more at other times.

PHOTO COURTESY OF I. FRANCAIS

The importance of having a hide box in the enclosure cannot be overstated. Lack of secure hiding place will cause your leopard gecko severe stress.

Jade plants are bright green, thick-leafed succulents that are very common as house plants. They get large, but are slow-growing, so a small specimen can make a nice accent in your leopard gecko cage. They need good soil but good drainage as well and should be watered but not drenched about once a week.

Snake plants, *Sanseveria* species, have broad, leathery leaves. There are both large and small varieties and many different colors including some attractive variegated ones. Medium light, moderate water.

Aloes are the plants that everyone keeps to break off pieces of to rub the sap on minor cuts and rashes. They are good terrarium plants too. A mixture of soil and grit will keep them healthy. Bright light, moderate water. *Haworthia* are similar in appearance and care.

The above plants are not the only ones you might consider. There are plenty more at your local nursery. Look around. You can either leave them in their pots, which can usually be hidden by artfully placed rocks, or you can plant them permanently in the terrarium.

I should also mention that there are now some very nicely crafted artificial cacti and succulents that are made for reptile terrariums. They are made of ceramic or plastic, and you really have to look twice to see that they're not real. If you like the look of plants but don't have a green thumb, or would rather not deal with live plants because they cannot be sterilized, these clever fakes may be for you.

LIGHT, HEAT, HUMIDITY

Okay, we're almost done. We've laid out the substrate, placed the hidebox or other shelter, and

PHOTO COURTESY OF G. &. C. MERKER

Do not be alarmed if you see your gecko eating its shed skin; this is a normal behavior.

arranged whatever other decorations are attractive. Now place a tight-fitting screen top on the cage. Yes, I know that leopard geckos can't climb glass, but sometimes they can stand on top of a rock and/or scritch up into a corner and get enough leverage to get a leg up over the tank rim and climb out. It's a remote possibility, but why take the chance?

Once the lid is in place, use an incandescent light above the cage to create a basking area inside. There are gooseneck and clip-on lamp fixtures for reptiles that you can get at your pet shop. A incandescent "spot" bulb of 60 or 75 watts should be sufficient to raise the temperature of a rock or area of substrate to about 87-90°F. This should be at the opposite end of the terrarium from the shelter

Hatchling albino leopard gecko. The care of albinos is no different than the care of normal individuals.

PHOTO COURTESY OF P. FREED

area. What this does is create a *thermal gradient.* This fancy term just means that the cage has a hot side and a cool side, and areas that are somewhere in between. This lets your lizard choose its own preferred temperature. As reptiles, lizards are "cold-blooded," but this term is really not accurate. Reptiles can have a body temperature hotter than yours or mine, but they don't generate the heat internally the way we do. They absorb the heat from their environment, and by shuttling back and forth between hot spots and cool areas, they can maintain a fairly steady body temperature. This is actually a pretty efficient way of doing things. It means that a reptile can use nearly all the energy it gets from food for growth, reproduction, and other functions. Mammals like us have to spend part of our energy "budget" on keeping our temperature up, which means we have less to use for other bodily functions.

The incandescent light will heat up the basking spot, but as you may have already thought, what good does it do if the light-shy geckos don't come out? The rocks and sand will hold the heat for some time after lights-out, but an alternate method of providing heat is to place an electrically heated "hot rock" in the terrarium. This is fine, as long as the rock doesn't get too hot. It often helps to bury the hot rock in the sand to spread the heat a little more. Use a thermometer to check. Remember, no higher than 90°F. Again, place this heat source at the opposite end of the cage from the hidebox.

Even if you use a hot rock, you'll need some kind of light source. Leopard geckos are nocturnal, and will hide when the

Patternless leopard geckos are often called leucistic, although this is not correct. True leucism would result in a pearly white animal.

PHOTO COURTESY OF E. LOZA

Photo by R. D. Bartlett, courtesy The Gourmet Rodent

Individuals with bright yellows and oranges and reduced spotting are all the rage in the leopard gecko hobby.

light is on, but the light is necessary nonetheless, because it lets the geckos set their internal "clocks." Except for periods of dormancy, the length of the terrarium "day" should be about 12 hours or a little more.

Some keepers of leopard geckos recommend full-spectrum fluorescent lighting, such as vitalites. These lights will help basking reptiles manufacture some of their Vitamin D, but since leopard geckos hide from the light, I think these lights are unnecessary. Use vitamin supplements in the diet instead.

Leopard geckos are desert animals, but their lairs often have a higher humidity than the surrounding habitat. Using a spray bottle to mist the cage once a day, particularly near the entrance to the lair, will help to elevate humidity levels. Don't get carried away. When I say "mist," I don't mean "drench!"

That's really about all there is to setting up a habitat for leopard geckos. There is only a little bit of regular maintenance, consisting mainly of removing fecal material and filling the water bowl with clean water daily.

FOOD AND WATER

Leopard geckos are not difficult to feed. In fact, they're about the easiest lizards I can think of when in comes to keeping them fed. They are insectivorous—insect eaters—and you can easily keep them on just one or two different types of insects.

CRICKETS

Crickets are going to be the staple diet you feed your geckos. The gray or house cricket, *Acheta domestica*, is available in just about any pet shop, and in a wide variety of sizes, from adult crickets over an inch in length to tiny nymphs (baby crickets, called "pinheads" in pet shop parlance).

Choosing the right size for your gecko is easy—just look at the lizard's head. The head of an adult gecko will be a bit over an inch long, and these lizards will take fully adult crickets. For smaller geckos, feed crickets no larger than the length of the lizard's head, and a little smaller if possible. A newly hatched gecko will need pretty small crickets, but you will not have to go all the way down to pinheads.

Crickets can be bred, but few hobbyists attempt it since they are so cheap to buy, so we won't go into the details here. You'll find it easiest if you buy a couple of dozen crickets at a time. However, DO NOT FEED THEM TO YOUR

Silkworms are one of the most nutritious insects to feed your leopard gecko. They are generally not sold at pet stores and must be purchased online.

PHOTO BY G. AND C. MERKER, COURTESY OF MULBERRY FARMS

GECKO ALL AT ONCE! Store them in a lidded container to keep them from climbing out. Most pet shops sell something called a "small animal cage," a plastic box with a slotted lid that clips on. These are perfect, but if you're economizing even a gallon jar will do. (Don't forget to punch holes in the lid.) Your two dozen crickets have pretty much emptied their digestive tracts and consist of little more than chitin (shell) and a bit of protein. Before you feed them to your geckos, they need to undergo a process we call "loading." What this means is that you want to stuff the crickets with nutritious food before you feed them to your lizards. That way,

PHOTO BY W. P. MARA

Crickets can be stored in many types of containers, but they should have some shelter, provided here by corrugated egg-carton cardboard.

should keep an adult gecko going for over a week, a little less for fast-growing youngsters.

But crickets, as purchased, are not really a complete meal. Pet shops buy them in bulk from breeders, but they sell so fast that the typical pet shop does not have the time to feed them. At best, the crickets have gone without food for at least several days when you buy them, and in that time they your gecko gets not only the cricket, but extra nutrition from whatever the cricket has eaten.

Crickets are not too choosy—they will eat almost anything. What we want to do is boost their protein content a bit, add some vegetable bulk, and raise the levels of several important vitamins. There are several foods to do the job of adding protein. Various rodent foods, if ground to a powder, will suffice, but I prefer to use tropical fish flake food, most of which are over 50% protein. All this dry food will get the crickets pretty thirsty, so also provide a small piece of juicy fruit or vegetable (this will also help to boost their vitamin and mineral

but it really is worth the effort. Don't forget, the cricket is only the "package" for all this good stuff—it's really food for the gecko, and a gecko that gets a balanced diet will be active, strong, and a good breeder (more on that later).

PHOTO BY M. GILROY.

The gray or house cricket, *Acheta domestica*, is a staple food for leopard geckos.

Okay, you've patiently waited while the crickets enjoyed their last meal, and now it's dinnertime for your gecko. Whoa! Not quite! There is one final step; again, we're going to boost the nutritional value of the crickets. Just before you offer them to your gecko, dust the crickets with a vitamin/mineral powder made specifically for reptiles.

content). Two good choices are shredded carrot (provides vitamin A and some calcium) and slices of orange (also a good calcium source, and provides lots of vitamin C). You can also try cubes of summer squash, some cantaloupe or other melon, and all sorts of other veggies. Always give the crickets the dry rodent or fish food, but alternate the vegetables—give carrot to one batch of crickets, orange to the next batch, etc. "Load" the crickets for at least 12-24 hours before you offer them to your lizard(s).

I know that providing gourmet meals to crickets was not exactly the first thing you had in mind when you bought a leopard gecko,

That last bit is important: "...made specifically for reptiles." Without getting technical about it, let's just say that different groups of animals absorb vitamins and minerals in different forms, and a vitamin supplement suitable for a mammal (like the daily multivitamin you take) may NOT be suitable for reptiles. Your pet shop should be able to supply you with a suitable reptile vitamin supplement, but read the label to make sure of one especially vital factor—at least a 2:1 ratio of calcium to phosphorus. In other words, there should be at least twice as much calcium as phosphorus in the mix. If this isn't the

PHOTO BY C. O. MASTERS.

Mealworms, the larvae of a beetle, are good for leopard geckos if not fed exclusively.

case, the phosphorus may actually interfere with calcium uptake. It's a delicate balance. (While you're checking these other things on the label, check the expiration date too.)

So dust the crickets with the vitamin powder (I find it easiest to just place them in a ziploc bag and "shake-and-bake"), and NOW you're ready to feed your gecko.

MEALWORMS

The lowly mealworm is another staple of herp-keepers. *Tenebrio molitor* is actually a small black beetle, and the mealworm is its larva.

The mealworm has recently fallen on hard times as a herp food item, but that is probably unfair. As with any other herp food, there's a right way and a wrong way to utilize it. The people who give mealworms a bad rap say that they're high in chitin, and the problem with chitin is that it's indigestible. Some herps that have been fed mealworms exclusively develop digestive problems, especially a tendency to pass whole mealworms through the tract undigested. This usually only happens when the herp is literally stuffed with mealworms, or when the mealworms are too large for the animal. In other words, don't feed big adult mealworms, which are a little over an inch long, to a baby leopard gecko. Full-grown geckos, on the other hand, can easily handle even the largest mealworms.

You can decrease the amount of chitin your gecko ingests be feeding only softshell (freshly molted) mealworms, which have not yet deposited much chitin in their exoskeletons. The softshells are easy to spot—they're white, and the "hard" mealworms are an amber-brown.

You can easily raise mealworms in a container of dry rolled oats with a couple of slices of potato added. The depth should not be more than a couple of inches. Fungal infections can quickly wipe out a mealworm colony if the oat/potato mix is damp. The larvae, pupae, and adult beetles can all be kept together, and before long you will notice new baby mealworms crawling through the mix. About a day before offering them to your gecko you can place them in a separate container with some slices of apple, orange, or banana, or small piles of shredded carrot, in order to "load" them as you did the crickets. The final stage should be to dust them with vitamin/mineral supplement.

KING MEALWORMS

A fairly recent addition to the herp keeper's pantry of live foods is the so-called "king mealworm," *Zophobas* sp. These are big critters compared to normal mealworms—they reach about an inch and a half as larvae. They are only suitable as food for full-grown leopard geckos, and the same restrictions apply as with the smaller mealworms—in other words, don't feed too much.

You can raise the king mealworms in an oat-and-potato medium, just like their small cousins, but there is one important difference: they will not go into the pupal stage (the inactive "cocoon" stage just before the adult beetle merges) if you leave them "in the mix." However, if you take a big larva out of the culture box and put it in a small container by itself, within a few days to a week the transformation will occur. Repeat as necessary, and you'll have the adult beetles you'll need to start the next generation of kings.

WAXWORMS

The waxworm is not a worm at all, but a small caterpillar—the larva of a moth. Waxworms infest old beehives, feeding on the wax and honey within. They are an excellent food for adult geckos if fed sparingly, as they are a bit on the rich side. However, they are an excellent food for getting mature female geckos into breeding condition, since the extra fat is needed for the production of egg yolk.

Waxworms are not the easiest of live foods to get your hands on, but you should be able to find them at a pet shop that caters heavily to the herp market. If this doesn't pan out, you can sometimes get them through beekeepers or suppliers of fishing bait. It is best to buy them as needed, but if you can only get them in bulk you will need something to feed them. Real honeycombs are the best, but you can also use a mixture of honey, wheat germ and a good pinch of yeast, to which are added equal amounts of cornmeal and poultry mash until you have a firm paste. And as usual, don't forget to dust!

PHOTO BY K. T. NEMURAS.

A leopard gecko lapping water from the surface of a leaf. Unlike some other pet lizards, leopard geckos will drink from a water bowl.

PINKIES

Pinkies are hairless baby mice. Mice? But leopard geckos are insectivores, right? In general, yes, but we will make this one exception, because pinkies are an excellent food for adult geckos, especially geckos you want to breed. If you asked a randomly selected group of leopard gecko breeders to name one secret to getting their geckos into breeding condition, I'll bet most would say "Pinkies!"

The reason pinkies are such a good food is that they are a self-contained package of good nutrition. The liver and other internal organs of the small mice are very nourishing for your lizard. You don't have to "load" them as you do the insects, though it does help if you dip their rumps in the vitamin supplement.

Pinkies are best fed live, at least until your gecko becomes accustomed to this food item. Their squirming motion is very attractive to a gecko. Some lizards will eventually learn to take thawed frozen pinkies from your fingers, but until then, feed live ones if

Leopard geckos often become tame enough to take food from their keepers' fingers. Here one accepts a "pinkie" mouse.

possible.

I can understand it if you're a bit squeamish about using pinkies to feed your lizard. We humans don't get very upset when a bug buys the farm, but somehow it seems different when it's a warm-blooded little creature like a baby mouse—after all, we're mammals too. But there's no cruelty involved here—it's just predator and prey, and leopard geckos really do dispatch their prey very quickly and efficiently. This is just the way life works—it's not good, it's not bad, it just *is*.

HOW MUCH, HOW OFTEN

Hatchling and small juvenile leopard geckos are growing very fast, and so you need to get a lot of food into them. I recommend feeding them on a daily basis. Four to six crickets or small mealworms will likely be enough, but watch your lizard's behavior to fine-tune your feeding schedule. If it eats all the insects very quickly, offer a couple more. If it eats several and then slows down and seems to lose interest, try offering a couple fewer insects next time.

Large juveniles in the 6-inch range can take large crickets or the largest common mealworms. Offer them in roughly the same numbers as above, but only every other day.

Adults need only be fed two to three times a week, except when you are conditioning them for breeding, in which case you should feed them every other day or even every day as egglaying draws near (see the chapter on breeding for more details). King and regular mealworms, full-grown crickets, and a weekly pinkie will keep your gecko in really first-class shape.

If you have any doubt as to whether your gecko is getting enough food, weigh it on a regular basis. A newly hatched gecko tips the scales at 3-4 grams, while a healthy non-breeding adult should weigh a bit over 50 grams. Speciments almost twice this heavy are known, but this would be considered abnormal. As with many captive herps, obesity is a danger, and can lead to fatty liver degeneration and other ills. All herp keepers walk a constant tightrope between "too little" and "too much" when it comes to feeding. I hope the above tips will help, but if there's one bit of advice I can give that overrules them all, it's this: WATCH YOUR ANIMALS. Don't just watch, but OBSERVE. There are subtle behavioral changes that will let you know what to do if you're alert. I can't tell you exactly what I mean, but it's sort of like the gardener's "green thumb," an intuitive way of doing things. Well, herp keepers have a "scaly thumb" (sorry, that's the best I could come up with). Watch and learn.

WATER

I'll bet you thought I forgot about this, right? Leopard geckos originated in a dry habitat, but they do need a fair amount of water. Unlike some desert lizards, which can manufacture water internally from the foods they eat, leopard geckos need drinking water. In the wild I imagine they drink dew, which does exist in all but the driest of habitats.

Providing water for some captive lizards can be a bit of a hassle, since many will not drink from a water dish. Fortunately, that's not the case with leopard geckos. Give them a dish of water and they'll find it when they need to drink, about every other day or so. I recommend providing fresh water at all times, and every day you should take out the bowl, rinse it, and add clean water.

The water bowl should be small

and shallow, about 3 inches in diameter and about a quarter-inch deep, with straight sides. A laboratory petri dish is perfect. Your pet shop may have them, but if not you can get them from a surgical supply store or a biological supply catalog. You can even improvise your own water dish, but—and I can't stress this strongly enough—make sure it's not so big and deep that your gecko could fall in and drown.

Geckos are creatures of habit—and sometimes they develop bad ones. An occasional gecko will routinely defecate in the water dish, and if this is the case you should not provide it with a water dish at all times. Either provide the dish only when you can watch them drink, and then remove it, or train them to drink from an eyedropper. Most can learn to do this pretty quickly.

Good food, good water. Add that to a terrarium with the proper conditions and shelter, and you have the makings of healthy leopard geckos.

BREEDING

Once you have gotten pretty good at the day-to-day aspects of leopard gecko maintenance, I would be very surprised if you were not interested in breeding them—especially considering that it's so easy.

If you raised your own geckos from babies, they will be easy to sex at about one year of age. The easiest way to sex leopard geckos is to grasp them gently in your hand and turn them over. Males will have a row of dark-colored preanal pores just ahead of the vent. Females also have these pores, but they are much smaller and usually the same color as the surrounding scales, so they are nearly invisible. Another giveaway is that males have a pair of swellings at the base of the tail, just behind the vent. These are called *hemipenile bulges,* and are the external signs of a pair of pouches that house the twin lobes of the male's penis. (Many people think that male lizards and snakes have two penises, but that's not quite accurate.

A leopard gecko grasping a pinkie mouse. Pinkies should not be fed to these lizards too often, but are useful for conditioning them for breeding or as an occasional treat. Photo by J. Merli.

They really do have just one organ, but it is split into two sections, joined at the base. Each half is called a *hemipenis*.) Some breeders claim that males and females can be distinguished by body form as well, with males being a little bigger and thicker in build. I wouldn't trust this method, though. Leopards of both sexes are variable in build, and a lot depends on how well they have been fed. If this is your first attempt at breeding leopard geckos, stick with looking for pores/bulges to find the males.

I should also mention that some breeders can spot the pores and bulges at much earlier than one year, but it takes practice. This means looking at lots of geckos. If you want to be a little more sure of you diagnosis, use a small hand lens to give you a bit of magnification, and maybe even show your geckos to an experienced breeder or the herp person at your pet shop.

But even after you've determined the sexes of your geckos, they are not quite ready to breed. Notice that I said they're *sexable* at one year, not *mature*. There's a difference! One-year-old leopard geckos will probably mate successfully, but most are still too young to produce viable eggs and sperm. They may mate and then no eggs are produced, or the female may lay infertile eggs. The age at which the geckos are both sexable and sexually mature is about 18 months. Don't rush things. Forcing immature geckos to try to reproduce may

PHOTO BY J. MERLI.

A pinkie mouse is quite a mouthful, and should only be offered to fully adult leopard geckos.

occasionally produce offspring, but it also needlessly stresses your breeders and can lead to early death.

Obviously, if you don't want to be bothered with sexing geckos yourself or with waiting for babies to grow into breeders, you can always buy fully mature and sexed adults from your pet shop. They will cost quite a bit more than babies, but if you want to get into the breeding game quickly, it's an option.

Okay, so let's say you've obtained your breeder geckos, one way or the other. How do you get them together?

First, pick the right time of year. Leopard geckos often show some sensitivity to the change of seasons, even in captivity. They most often breed from about February to September. While it is possible to get them to breed even in the dead of winter, it is easier to follow their natural seasonal patterns. So, beginning in December, decrease the photoperiod (day length) to about 6 hours, and also decrease the temperature about 10°F overall. What you're doing is reminding the lizards that it's winter, and time to rest. You will find them more sluggish and eating less during this period. After about eight weeks of this, gradually bring the temperature back up and increase the photoperiod to ten to twelve hours. Get it? It's "spring" now. Start feeding the lizards heavily, and don't neglect the calcium supplements, especially for the female—she'll need it shortly to produce eggshells.

Many breeders of leopard geckos keep their adults in individual cages except for short periods when they are brought together to mate. If this is your approach, now is the time to select a robust male and a nice fat female. If you want pretty offspring, try to pick specimens with bright colors and distinct, crisp patterns.

Place the female into the male's cage. Since you have recently revived the lizards from their winter rest, the male should get excited quickly, and the female should be receptive. The male will approach the female with body held high, tongue flicking to catch her scent, and tail twitching. He will pursue her if she runs, but if she does not he will attempt to mate almost immediately. Do not be concerned if you see the male approach the female from the

PHOTO BY M. GILROY.

Leopard geckos feed primarily on insects such as this locust. In captivity, crickets are the best staple food.

PHOTO BY J. MERLI.

A female leopard gecko and two eggs in her nesting box. Leopard geckos almost always lay two eggs.

A hatchling leopard gecko just breaking free of its egg.

PHOTO BY I. FRANCAIS, COURTESY OF BILL BRENT.

side and bite her on the nape of the neck. This is a common maneuver in many lizards, and it holds the female still while the male gets into position. Side-by-side, the male now wraps his tail under the female's so that their vents meet, and wraps his hind-legs around her pelvis. When he's in position and the female is holding still he inserts one hemi-penis into her oviduct. The lizards are still now as sperm is transferred, and separate after-wards. Mating is now completed, and you can now return the female to her cage.

Over the next several weeks you will see the female get in-creasingly heavier because of her developing eggs. She will start looking slightly lumpy, and if you turn her over you will actu-ally see the outlines of the eggs through her slightly translucent skin. She will get restless, roam-ing about her cage as if in search of something. She is—a place to lay her eggs.

At this time, place into her cage a lidded plastic container that is partially filled with damp (not wet!) sphagnum moss. An old margarine tub works well, but a rectangular container about 8 x 6 x 1.5 inches deep is roomier. Cut a hole in the top large enough to admit the female, and bury the box so that the top is level with the substrate. This

Juvenile leopard geckos have a banded pattern. The bands usually break up into spots as they grow, but some adult leopards retain traces of the bands.

PHOTO BY W. MUDRACK.

PHOTO BY K. T. NEMURAS.

Leopard geckos often use their tongues to clean themselves.

humid "cave" is just what the female is looking for, and you should check it every day to see if the female has laid her eggs, which are oval and about an inch long. She will probably lay two eggs, although a very young or very old female may lay just one. Three eggs are virtually unknown. Remove the eggs for incubation. (More on this in a minute.)

After a couple of weeks of rest, you can mate the female again, if you like. While it is true that female leopard geckos lay only two eggs per clutch, they can lay up to six clutches per season. Be aware, though, that females that are forced to produce the maximum number of clutches per season may be shorter-lived than those that are allowed a bit more rest. You will get more offspring from your females in the long run if you mate them only 2-3 times a year.

The above method of breeding leopard geckos is very efficient, and it has the advantage of letting you keep very accurate records of the parentage of your hatchlings, which is vital if you are breeding toward a goal, such as increased color, larger body size, etc. The disadvantage is that it does require a lot of attention to detail. There is another way.

Some breeders take a more casual approach by placing one male with a "harem" of up to a half-dozen females in a large cage. These hobbyists usually omit the winter dormant period as well. This means the male can pick his own mate, as well as the time for mating. There are several disadvantages, however. One is that females, while far less aggressive than males, will sometimes fight, and even those that are not physically attacked may be intimidated to the point that they do not eat well. The male may also stress the females with unwelcome courtship advances at times when they are not ready to mate. Individual lizards also vary in their willingness to breed without the winter rest; some don't seem to care, and others will breed reluctantly if at all.

Make sure the enclosure is large—about 36 inches (the length of a 30-gallon aquarium)—and make sure there are adequate hiding places for each animal. Multiple hideboxes or plastic terraces will help to divide up the available territory. Still, keep an eye out for any lizard that might be getting beat up by its cagemates. Look for bite marks and missing toes or tails, and remove such individuals immediately for solitary recuperation. Leave an egg box in the cage constantly, and check it often—but also try to ensure that a dominant lizard does not take it over as his or her personal gecko condo. If you put the egg box in the cage only after the lizards have chosen other hiding places (give them a week or so), this will probably not be a problem.

Feel free to try the harem setup if you wish. Many amateur and professional breeders are fabulously successful with it, but a few fail completely. If things don't work out for you, switch to the more structured method we considered first.

We're almost there now. You've successfully mated your geckos, and the female has presented you with a couple of fine eggs. What now?

The eggs should now be removed from the box where they were laid and placed in a small plastic shoebox that is filled halfway with sterile damp sand or vermiculite. Vermiculite is the better choice. The shoebox will become our incubator. Place the eggs in the vermiculite in the same position in which you found them. If the eggs were stuck together it is best to leave them that way. If you try to separate them you could rip them open; it takes very little pressure to do so. If they were not stuck together, place the eggs about an inch apart in the incubator box. Bury the eggs halfway in the vermiculite. The lid of the shoebox should have a number of tiny holes drilled into it so that air can circulate, but it should not be drafty enough to let the eggs dry out. This is a difficult balancing act—too little air, and the eggs will develop fungus and rot; too much, and they will dry out.

The humidity balance is only half of the battle when it comes to incubating leopard gecko eggs. Temperature balance is the other half. The temperature for incubating leopard gecko eggs has to be between 80 and 90°F. And that temperature has to be con-

stant. Fluctuations are, well, bad.

Here's an interesting bit about the temperature balance. YOU can select the sex of your leopard geckos. Leopard geckos have "temperature-dependent sex determination." I call it the 80-85-90 rule. If you incubate your gecko eggs at a temperature of 80°F, almost all of the hatchlings will be female. At 85°F, they'll be about half-and-half. At 90°F,

PHOTO BY M. GILROY.

A hatchling leopard gecko. The slightly aberrant first dark band, which in this case has a teardrop-shaped marking intruding into it, is fairly common.

PHOTO BY R. D. BARTLETT.

This is not a juvenile leopard gecko, but a hatchling Tucson banded gecko, *Coleonyx variegatus bogerti*. The New World banded geckos are close relatives of the Old World leopard gecko, and the resemblance is striking.

almost all the babies will be male.

A simple way to maintain both constant temperature and humidity within the incubator box is to employ an aquarium and a submersible heater. A 10- or 20-gallon aquarium should do, depending on the size of the shoebox. Place a couple of bricks inside the tank and then fill the tank with about 3 inches of tepid water. Place a fully submersible 50-watt aquarium heater horizontally in the aquarium. Make sure it is completely underwater. Place the incubator box on top of the bricks. There should be about an inch of air between the box and the water. Plug in the heater and begin to adjust the temperature. Finally, cover all but a small slit at the top of the aquarium with a plastic top or a sheet of plastic wrap. This will help to hold in both heat and humidity.

You will need an accurate thermometer, but do NOT measure the water temperature. Measure the temperature INSIDE the shoebox. Keep adjusting the heater upward until the temperature inside the box has reached the desired temperature and is holding steady. This can take several days.

You may have already guessed, since I said that temperature fluctuations are bad, that your best bet would be to assemble and adjust the aquarium incubator setup BEFORE you need it. Sometimes eggs appear as a "surprise" when you least expect them, but most of the time you should have enough lead time to get the incubator ready.

There are at least a couple of other incubator options that have some merit. Some reptile

A more recent innovation is a thermostatically controlled heated shelving unit that holds a couple of dozen plastic shoeboxes. This can be useful for incubation of a large number of reptile eggs and even for housing a colony of juvenile or adult leopard geckos.

Leopard gecko eggs will hatch in about six to ten weeks, depending on the temperature;

PHOTO BY R. D. BARTLETT, COURTESY THE GOURMET RODENT

A spectacular captive-bred leopard gecko. Specimens with interesting patterns and especially bright colors may cost a few hundred dollars.

breeders use modified poultry incubators, and there are a few new incubators on the market that are designed specifically for reptiles. Check with your pet shop to see what is currently available.

development is faster at higher temperatures. Check the incubator box temperature and the physical condition of the eggs a couple of times per week throughout the incubation period. Look for fungus (it looks

PHOTO BY J. GEE.

This incubator box contains snake eggs, but the setup would be the same for leopard gecko eggs: a shallow plastic box with a layer of damp vermiculite and the eggs buried about halfway.

"furry") on the surfaces of the eggs and reduce the humidity a bit if you see any. Remember, the substrate should only be damp, not wet.

The baby geckos will be about 3.5 inches long upon hatching and will weigh a scant 3 grams. Handle them very gently. Keep them warm and away from drafts. They will not eat until about a week after hatching, when they shed their skins for the first time. Don't worry—they have enough yolk remaining to get them through this time. When they do begin eating, they will take several-week-old crickets. (An easy size gauge is a lizard's head. Feed crickets ½ to ¾ the length of a baby gecko's head.) Make sure the crickets are gut-loaded and vitamin-dusted. Provide the baby lizards with clean water continuously.

Baby leopard geckos can be kept together in large communal cages until they have grown a bit, as long as they are all the same size. Smaller individuals may be bullied, and will grow slower. If you have the space, it is really best to give each hatchling a shoebox of its own. They will grow more quickly when they do not have to compete with their siblings for food. These rearing containers should be spartan. All you need is a layer of paper towel, a very small water dish, and a tiny hidebox.

HEALTH

Leopard geckos have relatively few health problems compared to a lot of other herps. In fact, I hope you never have to refer to this chapter. Still, forewarned is forearmed, so here are some of the problems known in leopard geckos, and their treatments.

MOUTH ROT

I have heard of mouth rot occurring in leopard geckos, but I've never seen it myself. The cause is usually that the lizard bruises its snout against something, and then the gums get infected. If left untreated it can spread to cover the whole inside of the mouth. It usually looks pretty nasty, with a lot of yellowish pus-like (caseous) material and a fair amount of blood in severe cases. If you catch it early, mouth rot responds well to cleansing of the area with hydrogen peroxide and then swabbing with Betadine (an iodine-based cream) or a topical antibiotic. Severe cases may require an antibiotic to be injected by a veterinarian. It's a good thing this is rare in leopard geckos—keepers of water dragons and iguanas are not so lucky!

Leopard geckos need a secure hiding place to prevent stress. This lizard peers out from a hollow log.

PHOTO BY K. T. NEMURAS.

This leopard gecko is relatively dull-colored, being a mostly brownish ground color. Most breeders are attempting to increase the amount of yellow color, and many individuals have bright yellow even on the head. Photo by M. Gilroy.

SKIN INFECTIONS

If a leopard gecko is kept on a substrate that is badly soiled, especially if it is too moist, bacterial skin infections may result. This especially common on the belly, because it is directly in contact with the substrate most of the time. The infections appear as brown or black spots of varying size. The delicate toes are also commonly affected. The gecko should immediately be transferred to a sterile hospital terrarium with only a heat source, hide box, and water dish. The infected spot should be swabbed with Betadine or an antibiotic cream such as Neosporin or Polysporin.

MOLTING PROBLEMS

Sometimes a leopard gecko will have trouble shedding its skin. When I've watched leopard geckos molt, they generally complete the process in 45-90 minutes, and manage to remove all the old skin and eat it. If your gecko develops patches of molting skin that hang on for days, the problem is usually that the lizard is

PHOTO BY H. HANSEN.

When they feel secure in their surroundings, leopard geckos will often venture out to absorb heat ventrally from rocks. They may even nap, as this one is doing.

too dry. Get an old margarine tub and place some damp paper towels and the gecko inside. (Don't forget to punch holes in the lid!) Make sure not to let the lizard get cold during this process, or a respiratory infection could result. In most cases the humidity will loosen the skin so that the gecko can finish removing it within 24 hours. Always watch the toes! This is one place where old skin frequently hangs on and can cause infections later.

TICKS AND MITES

These external parasites are annoying but are rarely fatal. Still, they can carry diseases, and they can spread to every herp cage in your collection, so you want to deal with them immediately if you find them. The time-honored method of dealing with these pesky little arachnids was to hang a piece of no-pest-strip insecticide inside the terrarium, out of reach of the herps. Unfortunately, the insecticide in these strips has now been banned, so don't use them, even if you can find them.

There is, fortunately, a safe alternative. Under various trade names, you can now obtain a synthetic pyrethrin spray made for reptiles. Pyrethrin is a plant-based natural insecticide. The synthetic seems to be as safe as the real thing, and just as effective. Simply hold the lizard and spray it generously with the pyrethrin, being careful not to get any in the eyes or nasal openings. Then, immediately

PHOTO BY G. DINGERKUS.

In this juvenile, notice that the dark bands have begun to break up into black spots, and that spots are also appearing in the light bands. This gecko could be said to be a "teenager," and is probably 8-12 months old.

The popularity of the leopard gecko has created interest in other eyelid geckos. One that has recently become available in small numbers is the Nicaraguan banded gecko, *Coleonyx mitratus*. Only time will tell if this species will get established in the herp hobby. Photo by R. D. Bartlett.

rinse off the spray with cool water, and let the lizard dry completely in a warm place before placing it back into the display terrarium. One application is usually all that's needed.

DIGESTIVE DIFFICULTIES

Diarrhea, or more specifically, gastroenteritis, is a serious problem. Left untreated, it can quickly dehydrate a leopard gecko. Fecal oddities, such as watery feces with mostly undigested food, bloody feces, or green feces, are the danger signs. An afflicted gecko may also stop eating. The problem is that there are several different types of bacteria and protozoans that can cause this condition. Oral antibiotics are usually used in treatment, but knowing which one to use is difficult without

death. There are two ways to deal with this problem. First, make sure your gecko is getting enough food—don't forget to "load" those crickets and make sure you are using vitamin/mineral supplements as directed. Second, make sure that you are using a fine grade of sand (assuming that's your substrate of choice), as fine sand is less likely than coarse to cause gut blockage.

INTESTINAL WORMS

Flukes (flatworms), tapeworms, and nematodes (roundworms) are common intestinal parasites of reptiles. It is not impossible to find these parasites in leopard geckos, but since most of the geckos sold today are captive-bred, the worms are rare. A wild-caught gecko may carry a moderate to heavy load of these parasites. A captive-bred leopard gecko can also acquire worms through contact with the fecal material of wild-caught geckos or other lizards. Luckily for us, in many cases a particular worm's life cycle requires an intermediate host, usually an invertebrate. In other words, it can't just leapfrog from lizard to lizard.

The symptoms of a worm infestation can closely mimic those of gastroenteritis caused by bacteria or protozoans—poor or no appetite, weight loss, and fecal abnormalities. How do you tell the difference? In most cases, *you* can't. Adult worms or noticeable sections of them are only occasionally passed with the

knowing for sure what disease organism you're dealing with. It may be necessary to get your gecko to a vet who can take a stool culture and determine the proper drug to clear up the problem. Just remember, time is of the essence here.

Leopard geckos with dietary deficiencies, especially a shortfall of calcium, will eat a lot of sand, as mentioned earlier, and this can block the gut and lead to

PHOTO BY I. FRANCAIS, COURTESY OF BILL BRENT.

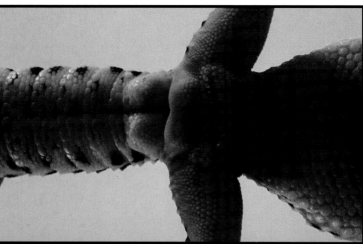

Above: The underside of a male leopard gecko, showing preanal pores and hemipenile bulges.
Below: An incredible leopard gecko with reduced spotting and intense yellow color. "High yellow" specimens are the goal of many breeders.

PHOTO BY I. FRANCAIS, COURTESY OF BILL BRENT.

feces. Most of the time the feces contain only microscopic eggs, and it takes an expert to find these. In other words, you need to take a stool sample to the vet.

Herp hobbyists are increasingly coming to the realization that only a vet can properly treat some herp health problems, and more vets are wise to the fact that herps are popular pets, and so they're willing to treat them. If you have a disease problem that you can't deal with, please find a vet who can. You've invested a lot of time in caring for your leopard gecko or other herp, so why throw it all away by risking your pet's life to your own amateur diagnosis? In the case of most external problems—mites, injuries, and so forth—you can easily take the proper steps, but with most internal problems you'll be guessing, at best.

CALCIUM DEFICIENCY

The extreme form of calcium deficiency is a condition called metabolic bone disease. It is most common in fast-growing juvenile geckos if they do not get enough vitamin/mineral supplements. The jaws get soft and the limbs may become distorted. What's happening is that the gecko is robbing its own bones of the calcium it needs for metabolism. The dietary problem is easily corrected, but any deformities are probably permanent. I hate to sound rough here, but if you have a problem with metabolic bone disease you have only yourself to blame, because only by not paying attention to a gecko's diet can the disease appear.

INJURIES

The most common sort of injury in a leopard gecko is a lost tail. If the injured animal is in a communal setup, immediately get it into a terrarium by itself. Swab the area with one of the disinfectants mentioned above, and watch for any signs of infection. Make sure that the lizard is extremely well fed and has plenty of water as well, so that it can quickly regenerate its supplemental storage organ.

PREVENTION

I really didn't want this chapter to be too much of a downer, because I really doubt you'll need most of this info if you followed my advice in the previous chapters. A clean and warm terrarium, good vitamin-supplemented food, and attention to the initial selection process will all ensure a healthy gecko that will never need any kind of disease treatment. The old cliche says that "prevention is nine-tenths of the cure," and there is really a lot of truth to that.

A view of the underside of a gravid female leopard gecko. Note that the outlines of two eggs can be seen. Proper calcium supplementation at this time is vital.

PHOTO BY I. FRANCAIS, COURTESY OF BILL BRENT.

PHOTO BY R. D. BARTLETT.

Among eyelid geckos, the African fat-tailed gecko, *Hemitheconyx caudicinctus*, is second only to the leopard gecko in terms of popularity. This is a juvenile.

An adult African fat-tailed gecko with a white dorsal stripe. Striped fat-tails are popular with keepers and breeders.

PHOTO BY K. T. NEMURAS.

OTHER EYELID GECKOS

Once you have had some experience with the leopard gecko, you may wish to try some of its "cousins" in the subfamily Eublepharinae. Let's look at a few of these geckos and how their care is similar to, or differs from, that of the leopard gecko. Keep in mind that the list below is far from a complete survey of the world's eublepharine geckos, but merely a glace at a few species that are common in the hobby as of this writing, or are interesting and unusual for other reasons.

AFRICAN FAT-TAILED GECKO, *HEMITHECONYX CAUDICINCTUS*

The African fat-tailed gecko is a species that is second only to the leopard gecko in popularity. It can reach virtually the same maximum size, about 10 inches, as the leopard gecko, but there seem to be more big fat-tails than leopards. Fattails are also a bit shorter-limbed and stouter of body when compared to leopards.

Fat-tails are very pretty animals, with alternating wide bands of chocolate-brown and

PHOTO BY M. PANZELLA.

Fat-tailed geckos are a bit more delicate than leopard geckos. A few wild specimens still appear in import shipments and must be acclimated gently.

beige. The eyes are dark, in contrast to the yellow-irised eyes of leopard geckos. An especially attractive variety of the African fat-tail has a dorsal white stripe. This is controlled by a simple recessive gene; in other words, if you mate two white-striped animals, all of their offspring will be white-striped as well. The white-striped fat-tails are preferred by breeders and hobbyists at the present time, but you will pay a bit more for them. Many breeders are also attempting to intensify the overall colors of fat-tailed geckos, and, some are seen with orange bands replacing the usual beige.

In general, the care of fat-tailed geckos is very similar to that of leopard geckos, but there are differences. Fat-tails do not like to be kept as dry as leopard geckos, and misting the cage lightly from a spray bottle once daily is beneficial. Molting problems are common in fat-tails that are kept too dry. To help retain humidity, some keepers prefer a fine grade of bark mulch to sand as a bottom covering. Regardless

Coleonyx elegans is a banded gecko from southern Mexico that is also available in very small numbers.

PHOTO BY R. D. BARTLETT.

A striped phase of *C. elegans*.

of what you use, however, cleanliness is more important than ever, because the higher humidity can promote disease if your substrate is soiled. The daytime temperature should be 85-90°F.

Fat-tails are often a little less docile than leopard geckos, and a big male can give you a good pinch, so leave them alone for the most part. Remember that all the eyelid geckos are "look at but don't touch" lizards, for their own safety and comfort. Get a corn snake if you have to have a reptile that likes to be handled!

African fat-tailed geckos are a bit tougher to breed than leopard gecko, and more than one breeder has been frustrated by them after having had an easy time with leopard geckos. Infertility is the most common problem, with females laying clutch after clutch of eggs that don't hatch. The solution? Patience! First of all, don't use the "harem" setup so common with leopard geckos. Keep the sexes separate except when you bring them together to mate. The winter period of semi-hibernation cannot be omitted. Finally, make sure your potential breeders are in absolutely tip-top shape, parasite-free and fattened up. Feeding the females heavily with calcium-dipped pinkie mice often

PHOTO BY K. LUCAS.

A male banded gecko, *Coleonyx variegatus*. Banded geckos are smaller and far more slender than leopard geckos, but their care is virtually identical.

works wonders. Finally, once you do get eggs, watch the incubator conditions carefully. Fat-tailed gecko eggs are a bit thin-shelled, and dry out more easily than leopard gecko eggs. The incubation temperature (80-90°F, optimally 85°) is the same as for leopard geckos, and evidence indicates that the same temperature-dependent sex determination applies.

The hatchlings are rather delicate, and must be kept individually. Make sure they are warm, and provide a hidebox and water dish. They do not feed right away. After their first molt, several days after hatching, they should start taking vitamin/mineral-dusted crickets and a few soft-shelled mealworms.

All eyelid geckos, such as this banded gecko, molt regularly, and usually eat the shed skin.

PHOTO BY A. KERSTITCH

PHOTO BY K. T. NEMURAS.

Banded geckos have an almost cat-like demeanor.

As of this writing many fat-tails are bred in captivity, but not quite as many as leopard geckos. Therefore, some wild fat-tails are still imported. These specimens are often dehydrated and carry impressive parasite loads. Avoid them if you can, but if you have no alternative or if you think a particular wild lizard is genetically valuable (a nice color pattern, for instance), make sure to have a vet do a fecal exam, examine carefully for ectoparasites and injuries, and keep the animal alone until it feeds well—and push the fluids!

BANDED GECKO, *COLEONYX VARIEGATUS*

There are eyelid geckos in the New World too. Usually these are all referred to one genus, *Coleonyx*. There are four species in the U.S., with more in Central America. The species most common in nature and most frequently seen in captivity is the banded gecko, *C. variegatus*. It ranges from the U.S. Southwest into Mexico, and has a number of subspecies (we won't consider them here).

Banded geckos are extremely variable, but in general they look a lot like juvenile leopard geckos except that the skin is smoother. Bands of dark brown alternate with equal-width bands of beige or yellow. The bands begin at the nape and run to the tip of the tail. Banded geckos reach a little over 4 inches, counting tail.

Banded geckos inhabit arid areas from true desert to dry forests. they are usually found in rocky outcroppings, and are fond of hiding by day under flat stones, such as those found in arroyos (dry streambeds). In captivity you can keep them in almost exactly the same way as leopard geckos, but a little drier and a few degrees hotter. They are too small to take even the smallest pinkies, so their diet should consist entirely of gut-loaded, dusted crickets and mealworms. Go light on the mealworms.

Banded geckos are fairly easy to breed by using the harem arrangement after a winter rest, but the hatchlings are very small and have to be started on wing-less fruitflies and "pinhead" crickets.

Banded geckos are charming little creatures, though virtually

PHOTO BY K. H. SWITAK.

Dark-colored rocks and blacktop roads absorb heat, and banded geckos can frequently be found in such places at night, their ghostly bodies a sharp contrast to the background.

PHOTO BY R. D. BARTLETT.

A very heavy reticulated gecko, *Coleonyx reticulatus*. This may well be a gravid female.

all those available are wild-caught. Perhaps it is only my own perception, but they do not generally seem to carry heavy parasite loads. You can collect them yourself by cruising desert roads at night. They often wander onto the warm blacktop of a paved road, and their pale color makes them stand out when hit by a bright light. Always make sure it is legal before you do any collecting! Although leopard geckos are common enough over most of their range to sustain light collecting without harm to the population, I hope that we will soon see captive-bred specimens as commonly as leopard geckos.

RETICULATED GECKO, *COLEONYX RETICULATUS*

Until 1956 this unusual gecko of the Big Bend region of Texas was unknown to science. In fact, the first known specimen was actually caught in a mousetrap. This is one of the largest New World eyelid geckos, and grows to just a hair under 7 inches. Reticulated geckos are brownish gray dorsally with fairly even dark spotting. There are large scales on the back interspersed with the fine, granular scales more typical of the genus.

They are found mostly along cliffs. (And let me tell you, Big Bend is full of cliffs and rocks, and hiking there can be painful-

PHOTO BY K. H. SWITAK.

C. reticulatus is sometimes called the Big Bend gecko because that rocky part of Texas is the only place where its range enters the United States. One of the largest New World eublepharines, it was unknown to science until 1956, and the first specimen was caught in a mousetrap!

—but that's another story!) Reticulated geckos squeeze themselves into cliff crevices, and have a semi-prehensile tail that helps them get around.

Relatively little is known about the details of keeping and breeding *C. reticulatus* in captivity. A smattering of them are collected by enthusiasts, but I don't know of anyone who has had long-term success with them. They seem to be quite delicate. If you really need to try, they should be kept in very rocky cages, but not too dry. Some people who have had poor luck were probably keeping them too dry. It may also be (and I'm just guessing here) that they need a large day/night temperature change. Depending on the season, spring being the most extreme, there can be as much as a 40°F temperature change from day to night in the Big Bend region.

TEXAS BANDED GECKO, *COLEONYX BREVIS*

Found in a broad swath on both sides of the Rio Grande, this 5-inch eyelid gecko is really not that unlike a small leopard gecko, as its bands tend to break up into spots as the lizard grows. They inhabit scrub and canyon-ion this is the most beautiful of our New World eublepharines, and I that's why I'm including it here. It is the second-largest New World gecko, at about 6.5 inches. It occurs in California and Mexico's Baja California. In California it is totally protected and collecting it is illegal, and I

The Texas banded gecko, *Coleonyx brevis*, does well in captivity. Unlike most of the other banded geckos, its bands almost always break up into spots, creating a lizard that looks very much like a miniature leopard gecko.

lands, and are typically found among flat rocks. They do reasonably well in captivity, and the conditions that apply to *C. variegatus* will keep *C. brevis* happy as well.

BAREFOOT GECKO, *COLEONYX SWITAKI*

Don't look at it, don't think about it, and for heaven's sake don't try to get one! In my opin-don't believe any are coming in from Mexico. Some herp hobbyists claim that California's shutdown on collecting *C. switaki* was a political move and had nothing to do with protecting the lizard. Certainly, California has been very anti-collector in the past.

The lizard is dark gray to blackish, with light bands on the tail and round white spots on the

PHOTOS BY P. FREED.

The desert is full of danger, and sometimes the predator can become the prey. Desert geckos—both the eyelid types and the non-eyelid types seen here—prey heavily on scorpions and spiders, but juveniles may be ambushed by the arthropods that would be a snack for an adult lizard.

Above: The San Diego banded gecko, *Coleonyx variegatus abbotti*. *C. variegatus* is an extremely variable species, and there are currently five described subspecies. Below: This Big Bend gecko looks distinctly uncomfortable in the bright sun. This species is still poorly known, and the few specimens that have been in captivity have not done well. The reasons are unknown.

PHOTO BY R. D. BARTLETT

PHOTO BY R. T. ZAPPALORTI.

PHOTO BY K. H. SWITAK.

A Texas banded gecko, *C. brevis*, collected at Big Bend. Though the ranges of *brevis* and *reticulatus* overlap geographically, little if any crossbreeding is apparent. Probably, differences in behavior, habitat, and even scent prevent the lizards from crossing.

body. The contrast is really quite striking, though California specimens are a little duller than the Baja animals.

Thanks to the ban, nothing is known about the captive care and breeding of this species. But we can dream, can't we?

JAPANESE LEOPARD GECKO, *EUBLEPHARIS KUROIWAE*

There are several subspecies of this fascinating but poorly known gecko from southern Japan. Some are nearly black in color (melanistic), while other subspecies and varieties are marked with bands or spots of pinkish beige. In all, the eye is an eerie ruby red. It has been found in forest and rocky regions, and at least some populations are fond of caves.

There are a few wild-caught specimens of *E. kuroiwae* available from time to time, though they command a pretty penny. Although there have been a few reports of captive breeding, no details are available. They are smaller and more lightly built than leopard geckos, but overall they seem easy to keep, their care being similar to that of leopard geckos except that a high humidity is necessary and they should probably be kept a bit cooler as well. These are very pretty geckos, and I'm going to go out on a limb here and say that I think they will soon become as common as leopard geckos. Only a few years ago, leopards were rare and expensive lizards in the hobby!

The barefoot gecko, *Coleonyx switaki*, ranges from southern California to Mexico's Baja Peninsula. Though attractive, it is strictly protected in California, and any legal specimens in captivity are in the hands of herpetologists with the proper permits. Photo by K. H. Switak.

PHOTO BY P. FREED.

Eublepharis kuroiwae orientalis, one of the subspecies of the Japanese leopard gecko. These geckos are sometimes placed in the genus *Goniurosaurus*.

MALAYSIAN CAT GECKO, *AELUROSCALABOTES FELINUS*

This rainforest gecko is one of the oddest critters in the whole bunch! Unlike the other eyelid geckos, which pretty much stay on the ground, this one is a climber. It can't climb walls, since like other eyelid geckos it lacks toe pads, but it can climb plant branches easily, though it does so with a slow, deliberate motion. It has a slender body, long toes, and a long tail that is probably prehensile. The head is very tapered and reminds me of an anole.

It is unfortunate that most of us will probably never see this unique gecko. Only a handful have ever been imported, and with import restrictions increasing, there may never be any

Head study of *Coleonyx mitratus*. Notice the enlarged scales that fringe the eyelids; these function much like eyelashes, to keep sand and other foreign objects out of the eye. Photo by R. D. Bartlett.

Another variant of *Coleonyx mitratus*. Photo by R. D. Bartlett.

more. Those that have been studied in captivity have been very delicate, prone to dehydration, and often heavily parasitized. Keeping a warm and humid terrarium without exposing them to skin infections will probably be a challenge. They are not easy to keep alive, and they have not yet been bred. I hope that will change, but I doubt it.

Facing page: Compare this head study of a Tokay gecko, *Gekko gecko*, with the head study of *C. mitratus* seen previously. Notice that the tokay also has scales fringing the eye, but there is not a hinge to make the eyelid movable. Thus, the tokay is not an "eyelid" gecko; its eyes are permanently open, but are protected by a transparent scale called a *brille* or *spectacle*. Photo by K. T. Nemuras.

Below: The Malaysian cat gecko, *Aeluroscalabotes felinus*, is an arboreal eyelid gecko that inhabits rainforests. Perhaps the oddest of its family, and one of the most primitive geckos alive today, it is almost unknown to hobbyists. This specimen is emaciated; the species appears to do poorly in captivity. Photo by M. J. Cox.

PHOTO BY P. FREED.

Above: *Coleonyx elegans* is relatively big-headed compared to other species in the genus.

Below: A very pretty juvenile *C. mitratus.*

PHOTO BY R. D. BARTLETT.

GLOSSARY

Autotomy—the ability of geckos and many other lizards to shed the tail when disturbed.

Eublepharines—eyelid geckos; a lizard subfamily that includes the leopard gecko.

Gastroenteritis—gastric disturbance caused by parasites and/or environmental stress; characterized by diarrhea.

Gecko—a lizard of the family Gekkonidae.

Hemipenile bulges—paired swellings at the base of the tail of leopard geckos caused by the male organ.

Hemipenis—one lobe of the penis in male lizards and snakes.

Herpetology—the study of reptiles and amphibians.

Herps—slang collective term for reptiles and amphibians.

Hidebox—artificial shelter for leopard geckos and other herps.

Photoperiod—day length.

Pinheads—slang term for newborn baby crickets.

Pinkies—slang term for newborn, hairless mice.

Preanal pores—a V-shaped row of dark pores, pointing forward, that distinguishes male eublepharine geckos.

Substrate—terrarium bottom covering.

The normal (no white dorsal stripe) form of the African fat-tailed gecko.

SUGGESTED READING

RD-800   *The Best Pet Reptiles*

RE-157   *The Guide to Plants for the Reptile Terrarium*

RE-168   *The Guide to Owning Geckos*

TS-166   *Keeping and Breeding Geckos*

YB-149   *Geckos Rare and Common*

LR-109   *Geckos*

RD-150   *Success With a Reptile Pet: Lizards Rare and Common*

RE-126   *Day Geckos: Keeping and Breeding them in Captivity*

RE-165   *Lizards; Keeping and Breeding them in Captivity*